DEVON P[RIVIES]

by

SHÂN TOYNE

COUNTRYSIDE BOOKS

NEWBURY · BERKSHIRE

COUNTRYSIDE BOOKS
3 Catherine Road
Newbury, Berkshire

ISBN 1 85306 511 0

Produced through MRM Associates Ltd., Reading
Typeset by Techniset Typesetters, Merseyside
Printed by Woolnough Bookbinding Ltd., Irthlingborough

CONTENTS

The Potty Privy Woman.

FOREWORD

Oh Moon, when I look on thy beautiful face,
Careering along through the boundaries of space,
The thought has quite frequently come to my mind,
If ever I'll gaze on thy glorious behind.

(Anon)

Devonshire is the biggest of the English counties after Yorkshire and Lincolnshire, and has the largest road network. In the process of researching for my privies I travelled over two thousand miles in Devon and discovered so much about this glorious area and its enormous variety of landscape. I feel I really know now why they call it God's Own County.

Though now *nearly* a Devonian having spent over thirty years here, my early childhood on the island of Anglesey, North Wales, with no electricity or running water and a Ty bach (little house) at the bottom of the garden probably gave me my life long fascination with the privy. I thought the fairies emptied the bucket and only years later discovered why my Nain (Welsh grandmother) had such a prolific vegetable garden. There is a lovely story of the insurance man knocking at the front door of a small Welsh cottage . . . small boy opens the door . . . 'Excuse me young man, is your mother in the Prudential?' 'Naw sir, she's in the Ty Bach.'

The outhouse or privy is fast disappearing, 'a victim of septics, sewerage and sophistication', and so I started my research by writing to all the local papers in Devon and to my delight every day for weeks the letters would arrive. Everybody over a certain age has a privy story, many of them unprintable. Letters were signed 'yours regularly'; it was hoped the book would be 'flushed with success'. Single-holers seemed easy but to my joy when glancing through the Properties for Sale in the *Western Morning News* I spotted a listed building for sale – with a listed three-seater privy. My first! We were off on the privy hunt . . .

For many folk in times past, the dunnekin, to give its proper Devon name, didn't bear thinking about. (Interesting thought: the Australians call them dunnies – might that have come from a Devonian sent down under for his nefarious deeds?) Polite people didn't refer to it *drekly*, as they say in these 'ere parts, and even those with a more basic outlook on life didn't dwell on the matter. Why is something that transcends class, colour and creed so smirked about? What after all do kings, beggars and poets have in common? I only hope the funny side of it all can be glimpsed in this little book.

A special thank you to Dido for her drawings, to Devon's Lord Lieutenant, Lord Morley, for giving me the title of the first chapter in this progress to the privy, and to my Devon Conservation Forum colleagues. Also, privies seem to bring out the muse in people and, although some marvellous compositions are included, I would love to have printed **all** the poems and prose I was sent. I would particularly like to express a big thank you to all the wonderful people in Devon who allowed us to invade their privacy and photograph their privies, and those who sent me photographs and/or anecdotes – the list is endless. We met and spoke to some remarkable and lovely people and without them this book would not exist and to all of them, whether we were able to use the material or not, I dedicate *Devon Privies*.

Last but no means least I am so very grateful to my husband Nico. All the photographs in this book are by him, unless otherwise stated, and I could never have begun to find all the locations without his map reading, driving, patience, and usual enthusiasm. He has had to put up with a lot, including the telephone call from a privy owner who said, 'I can't pronounce the name (Stan?) but do you know the Potty Privy Woman?' – Nico replied 'Yes, I am married to her.'

Talking of which, I make no apologies for the four letter words in this book for I am sure you would not be reading it if you couldn't call a spade a shovel!

SHÂN TOYNE

One photographer and tripod totally concealing the entrance to an ivy-covered privy at Wellesley Barton, Bishop's Tawton.

[1]

PRIVY COUNSEL

We've all got to go but where to go and then how to dispose of it has probably been uppermost, or should it be lowermost, in man's mind since cave dwelling days. It is an astonishing fact that we have only perfected the water closet or WC within the last 150 years. 'One small step for man – one giant leap for mankind' was the famous phrase spoken from the moon – yet for many in this septic isle the bucket in the privy was still our only form of sanitation. Many folk today under a certain age look quite blank when you talk of privies so before we journey round Devon visiting our privies of perfection let us venture back on this plumbers' progress.

The Palaeolithic caves at Torquay and Brixham show that in this isolated western area of Ancient Britain, prehistoric man was roaming. Neanderthal man had found shelter from the Ice Age in Kent's Cavern, Torquay. He needed water to drink and he would have found that running water carried away the family waste. It can't have been long before he discovered that his drinking water was more pleasant if taken upstream from the 'convenience' area – a very early beginning of sanitation but there were to be a few thousand years of suffocating odours to overcome before man began to be house-trained.

No progress seems to have been made until the Romans, leaving Nero at home in charge in AD 54, occupied Exeter as the most westerly of their towns in Britain. It is doubtful if they passed on details of any of their superior bathing and lavatory habits to the resident Celtic tribes of Dumnonnii. Some of their customs might well have put the local inhabitants right off, such as the little sponges on sticks that were used to wipe the Roman posteriors, rinsed if you were lucky, and passed on the next soldier in the twenty-seater latrine house. The Roman legions left our shores and in the course of time their villas were razed to the ground and our chance to learn about their plumbing vanished – we had lost a marvellous opportunity to clean ourselves up.

The earliest flush known appears to be Minoan. Pipes dating from 2000 BC, found in the Palace of Knossos in Crete, connected to a remarkably modern lavatory that may have had a wooden seat as well as a flushing water reservoir. Excavations have also uncovered an ancient Egyptian limestone keyhole seat with a removable pot in the pit below – a cold seat for a Pharaoh's bottom.

In Britain the monasteries were the guardians of sanitation. Cleanliness being next to godliness, this may explain why these establishments avoided the devastation of the Black Death in 1349. I found a wonderful description of the 'facilities' for the monks and novices at Durham: 'there were two great Pillars of Stone bearing up the whole floor thereof. Every Seat and Partition was of Wainscott, close on either side, so they could not see one another when they were in that place. There were as many Seats on either side as there were little windows in the Wall to give light to the said Seats ...' When you think that every moment of the day would have been worked out to a strict timetable, most of the brothers would need to 'go' at the same time; perhaps this is why there were many seats ranged either back to back or set against a wall. Imagine, if you will, the tolling of the monastery bell and the monks quietly filing to their reredorter (rere meaning 'rear' and dorter 'dormitory') and settling themselves in unison. Down below, with luck, would flow a stream, otherwise a stagnant moat. An odour of sanctity? On the Severn estuary at Tintern the tide was 'ingeniously employed to effect a complete flushing of the monastic dykes that must surely have swept them from their seats when the tide was highest'.

What a lovely name is 'reredorter'. It somehow sounds more fun than a toilet ... I spent some time as a very small girl at a convent school and we always had to ask to go to the 'vestiere'. Obviously our lovely nuns could not bear to use every day vulgar words for such every day normal habits and I now realise that we were basically asking to go to the wardrobe. There are so many modern coy euphemisms but even in medieval society you had the 'necessarium', 'the necessary house', and 'garderobe' (wardrobe). Hiding holes, priestholes and tiny private chapels found in grand houses were often in fact garderobes – there is even an

Nestling in the valley of the river Lew is an imposing Jacobean manor house with many fine panelled rooms. In one three-storey wing you can unhinge a large panel on each level and lo and behold a plain 'parlour stair' turret where chamber pots were placed behind the panelling for the servants to collect.

altar slab in a private chapel at Abington Pigotts, near Royston with a neat and bottom-sized circular hole in it. As for lavatory paper our monks were known to have torn up their old gowns, perhaps a little more hygienic than the Romans, but not much.

Garderobes in castles or large houses took the form of shafts, usually built in the thickness of a wall at the end of a right-angled passage (which was meant to trap the offensive smells). Astonishingly this may have worked, for a Dutchman visiting England in 1650 wrote: 'their chambers and parlours strawed over with sweet herbes refreshed me; their nosegays finely intermingled with sundry sorts of fragraunte floures in their bedchambers and privy rooms, with comfortable smell cheered me up and entirely delighted my senses'. The idea of these built-in privies was that everything dropped down the shaft to the ground below or the moat or stream – an unintentional and gruesome way of repelling boarders and probably more effective than boiling oil.

If the output did not fall into water there would have to be a pit which, in the course of time, would have to be emptied, by the 'gongfermors' or 'rakers'. Gong was a privy and fermor 'to fey' or cleanse. I wonder what they would be called today when you think that the good old rat-catcher is now a 'rodent operative'. One infamous gongfermor was 'Richard the Raker', who 'drowned monstrously in his own excrement' when the poor chap fell through the rotten seat of his privy in 1326.

The mountains of excrement must have piled high indeed for there is a fearful account of an occasion in 1281 when thirteen men took five nights to clear the pit of Newgate Gaol, for which they were paid £4 7s 8d. This was three times the going rate – but doesn't seem a lot for being up to your waist in putrid, smelling ordure . . .

The 'close stool' became the royal substitute for the garderobe and a royal retinue progressing from castle to castle would take a portable close stool/commode for the Sovereign, sometimes

A straight drop medieval privy with a useful pile of potential manure beneath it.

covered in lavish materials and lace. Hampton Court has a beautiful 'Royal Closet Stool' circa 1600 and inside the locked stool is a pot which some unfortunate courtier would have to empty. Samuel Pepys had a 'very fine close stool' in his drawing room.

A royal 'close stool', a stuffed horsehair seat covered in red velvet with two thousand gilt nails.

The rest of the court made do with a huge garderobe, one being said to have seated twenty-eight people. Greenwich Palace had a complicated system of courtyard urinals called 'pissing places' and, marked with red crosses, the idea was to encourage their use rather than the nearest corner.

Apart from Sir John Harington's remarkably unappreciated

water closet for his godmother, Queen Elizabeth I, in 1596, there wasn't much progress until the 18th century. Two hundred years ahead of its time, Sir John had invented a valve water closet which he described in his *Metamorphosis of Ajax* (a pun, for 'jakes' meant a privy). 'If water be plenty, the oftener it is used, and opened, the sweeter; but if it be scant, once a day is enough, for a need, though twenty persons should use it.' The Queen did have one built at her palace at Richmond but the Virgin Queen sounds none too clean as she is reported to have only had a bath once a month. She probably preferred to be enthroned on her cosy velvet covered close stool which the servants would be left to empty. That great writer of diaries John Evelyn, when he saw the splendid Versailles privies, remarked, 'To think that so much has been spent on beautifying a bogge'.

Devon doesn't appear to have had a privy champion but nearby Wiltshire did. The Revd Henry Moule, in the mid 1800s, was fed up with his smelly cesspool and discovered that by using a bucket and mixing the contents with earth the offensive smell was deodorised. The wooden seat, with bucket beneath, had a hopper at the back filled with charcoal, sieved ashes or earth. Perform the necessary, pull the handle and a layer of earth would pour onto the bucket, rendering the end product sterile and not at all offensive.

Some hundred and eighty years after Sir John Harington's *Ajax*, a London watchmaker, Alexander Cummings, took out the first 'valve closet' patent (1778) but unfortunately the valve wasn't very reliable. It took another Yorkshireman, Joseph Bramah, also the inventor of the hydraulic press, to improve on the valve design which became the standard for over one hundred years: a water closet with an S bend. Foul smelling sewer gases, lethal if ignited, were finally stymied by Cummings' invention of this 'stink trap' S bend which stopped them seeping back and into the house. At school I had a lovely dotty friend who was always cruelly known as Harpic because we thought

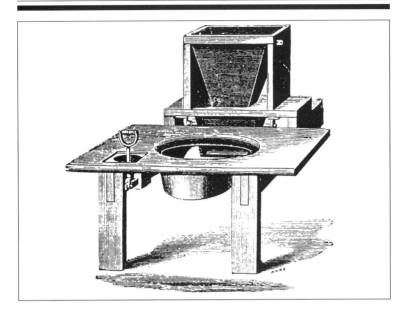

Reverend Moule's patented design.

she was round the bend. A 'bramah' came to mean anything of excellence and even today children playing conkers will refer to the best in their collection as a bramah and I bet they don't know the reason why.

No book on anything to do with privies could be complete without at least a mention of Yorkshireman Thomas Crapper, the inventor of their death knell (apart from those which survive through appreciation, neglect or necessity). In 1847 young Thomas was apprenticed at the age of 11 to a plumber in Chelsea. He eventually started his own business – Thos. Crapper and Co, Marlborough Works, Chelsea, a firm which didn't close until 1966 – and perfected 'Crapper's Valveless Waste Preventer, One Moveable Part Only, Certain Flush With Easy Pull, Will Flush When Only Two-Thirds Full'. His cistern, fitted to all water closets today, has the water flowing into it as soon as it

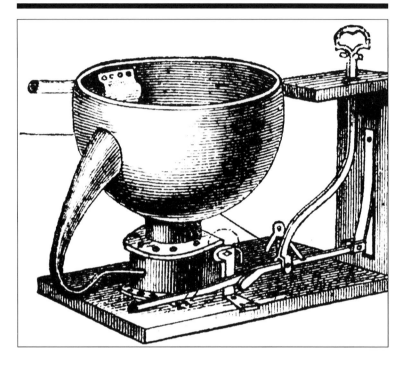

The accepted WC pattern for over a century after 1778 – what a bramah indeed!

is emptied by means of a floating ball on a metal arm which turns the water off when it rises to the top. Water remains safely in the cistern until the next person pulls the plug and lets it go. Most people have heard of Mr Crapper and perhaps seen his name printed on the back of a loo – but does he stay in our minds because it is believed he gave the English language the word 'crap'? Maybe its dictionary definition of 'nonsense, lies, exaggeration' is correct for the word was around some 700 years before young Thomas.

Inventor George Jennings' 'Pedestal Vase' was judged 'as perfect a sanitary closet as can be made'. Jennings installed public

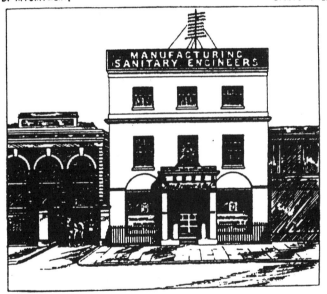
Mr. Thos. Crapper's showrooms – note 'By Appointment'.

17

A splendid Victorian pedestal vase.

lavatories at Crystal Palace for the Great Exhibition of 1851 and, probably for the first time, a charge was made. We owe the phrase 'spending a penny' to George, for the official report states that 827,280 people paid a penny each to sample those 'conveniences which nature demands'.

'Twas fine for the gentry and those who could afford these new-fangled contraptions, but privies certainly had not had their day . . .

[2]

PATH TO THE PROPER JOB

What about the workers? In spite of Victorian sanitary developments, the Devonian mineworkers, farmers and the rest of us still needed somewhere for the 'proper job' when the open fields didn't fit the bill.

Some dug a deep pit with a crude form of shelter over it, and the seat would be a plank with a hole. The liquid waste would seep away into the earth and the more solid matter would pile up and be used as fertiliser in the garden. Alternatively you just dug another hole. Layers of earth or ashes from the fire would be thrown in to dampen down the pong and some privies had an adjacent ash house built to make life a little easier.

Dry or vault privies were popular. If you made a solid base sloping slightly backwards any water would drain into the garden or farmyard through a small archway at the rear. Put a pile of earth against the arch and the solid waste couldn't escape. Wellesley Barton near Bishop's Tawton has been farmed by the Smith family for over a hundred years, though their listed farmhouse has been there for a couple of hundred years longer than that. Mr Smith was quite used to queries about his privy and told me that it had featured on television and in the *Daily Mirror*. The day we arranged to visit the whole family were out 'binding' on the farm but he gave me explicit directions on where to find his famous three-seater, some thirty yards away from the house. He had cleared the nettles and brambles, and some of the ivy so that we could get in. Very thoughtfully he had left us a roll of lavatory paper for the use of! The contents of this gem would have gone straight down to the midden behind but we didn't explore too closely for fear of upsetting the cows.

Depending on how many people were using an earth privy it would usually only be emptied when full, perhaps once a year.

Wellesley Barton's famous three-seater. Daddy Bear, Mummy Bear and Baby Bear?

This would be done from an opening at the bottom of the 'construction' with a long shovel shaped like a huge soup spoon and known in some circles as the 'shitthuss scoop'. For more on this breathholding subject please read the chapter on Privy Emptying.

The arrival of the bucket was good news for this prevented the frequently bottom-freezing draughts from the pit beneath. More often than not the same little building that had housed the earth privy was used. The pits, and some we saw were as deep as 7 foot, would be planked over, or even filled in with concrete, and the bucket placed under the same wooden seat (or seats). If there wasn't an opening at the back, or side, a trap door would have to be made in order to extricate said bucket when full. Often these buckets were of a rather special more conical design with an extra handle on the side. You jolly well needed that extra

To the right you can see the entrance to the privy which backs onto cows and the midden behind.

handle to balance the carrying when the bucket might be near to overflowing. On our privy hunt there would often be an exclamation of 'It's an earth one!' or 'It's a bucket and chuck it . . .'

But . . . first build your privy.

You didn't want your privy too far from the back door, for obvious reasons, so they were usually constructed a discreet distance away and preferably downwind. Build it of wood, brick, stone, cob or corrugated iron. White or lime-wash the inside, or paint it blue – for blue was said to ward off flies.

A good crunchy gravel path was a useful alarm for those sitting pretty at their business, who could then think of some way of warning those approaching that the privy was occupied. A lady in Holsworthy, that old market town in real midden farming Devon, kept geese in the back garden for they made wonderful natural burglar alarms and certainly advised any privy occupant that they were not alone!

Many privies had no fastening on the door – you held it shut with one foot and sang, whistled or coughed loudly – a simple answer to the modern 'engaged'. You might be lucky and find a big stone, or a house brick, inside either to wedge the door shut, or even hold it open in warmer weather. You could also use the stone as a foot rest, which was much more convenient than a stretched out leg. Alternatively you might have a simply designed latch or sneck, as do a lot of the privies in this book. (The dictionary definition of sneck is: 'the latch of a door or gate; the lever which raises the bar of a latch; a catch.' Hence sneck – to latch a door or gate – and a sneck-drawer is 'one who draws or lifts a sneck or latch in order to enter stealthily: a crafty, flattering, or sly fellow'!)

Ventilation was quite a speciality. At a basic level a 'modesty' door was all that was required. You could at least see from the path that the privy had someone in situ, and depending on the gap at the bottom, you could probably even tell who it was by the under garments on the floor. Alternatively a diamond or heart shape cut out at the top of the door would let the air in, or out, and often little birds likewise. Sweet smelling roses, honeysuckle and lavender grown near would help your nostrils cope with the smells but the elder tree helped to ward off the bluebottles and so did fennel.

The great majority of Devon privies had our native elder tree growing beside them or very close. Elder is known as 'The Witches Tree' and is surrounded by mystery and mythology. If hung over a doorway it certainly keeps out the witches – but it also helps to deter flies. Children would be taught to curtsy to an elder tree and to ask it politely before gathering its flowers, fruit or wood and then thank the tree for its gifts. Those who burn it are supposed to see the Devil. Legend says elders are in fact witches turned into trees by the saints but still able to cast a curse if you upset them. From early times the flowers, fruits, leaves, bark and roots have been used in herbal medicine. Herbalists still use all parts of the tree – elder leaf ointment is good for chilblains; elderflower and peppermint tea promotes perspiration and reduces temperature and it is also a mild stimulant. For those who considered alcohol unladylike, elderflower cordial was acceptable – and therapeutic. So always say please and thank you to an elder tree and, if no-one is looking, don't take chances, always curtsy.

Just as I was beginning this book we acquired e-mail at home and I was so excited when one of the very first we received was headlined 'Privvies'. Airline pilot Andy Markell said that we would be welcome 'at our convenience (sorry)' to take photographs and on a glorious sunny day we visited the Witheridge area and the Markells' beautiful home. There was what appeared to be the remnants of a privy, a few hundred yards away from the main house, but it had no 'furniture' left. There could possibly once have been a covered way leading to this privy. The *pièce de résistance*, however, turned out to be beside the entrance lodge and was probably the prettiest privy, and the only circular one, we found. Early 19th century with a conical slate roof and set over a stream, it was supposedly once a cosy two-seater. Access to the stream had been blocked off at a later date and it now contains, apart from the lawnmower, a plain wooden plank with a single hole with lid sitting over where a bucket once stood. In other words there had been a form of modernisation – to a point. Alfie, our dotty English setter, found it all very intriguing, as did Ian Bostridge, Master Thatcher. A true master of his trade, Ian has been responsible for thatching part of the new Globe Theatre in London. He was thatching away on the adjacent romantic little lodge and when I explained that I was writing a book about privies he told me his parents had just

Alfie doesn't understand – a circular building with a lawnmower and a seat and bucket!

bought a derelict row of cottages in Chawleigh – with privies.

Hereby hangs a tale . . . I had written to the ten District Planning Officers in Devon asking if they, or their Conservation Officers, would be kind enough to let me know if they came across, or knew of, any privies. They were unfailingly helpful (bar one) and I was thrilled when Michael Stocks from Mid Devon Dis-

Ian Bostridge, Master Thatcher, working on the delightful little lodge near Witheridge. The left-hand door conceals the circular privy.

trict Council telephoned me to say that he had just found a row of derelict thatched cottages in Chawleigh that had privies. He understood they had just been bought by someone and he couldn't find out who but hoped the cottages would be restored sympathetically. He was amazed that the cottages were not listed and immediately set about 'spot listing' them. The astonishing fact is that these Chawleigh cottages eventually turned out to be the very same ones that Ian Bostridge had mentioned his parents buying. I spoke some months later to Mr Bostridge senior who told me he had bought the cottages at auction on 11th July, completed on 24th July, and they were listed on 1st August!

The Secretary of State for Culture, Media and Sport is the grand title that appears, dated 1st August 1997, at the bottom of the new listed building schedule for the Chawleigh cottages. Seventeenth century, or even earlier, they were probably originally a three room cross-passage house which was later subdi-

25

The top half of this stable door at Chawleigh conceals a bucket privy with a wooden hay rack beside it. The big ditches are in preparation for a new drainage system.

vided into two cottages. We got there only just in time for there were big ditches being dug all around to install a drainage system. I have since learnt from the current owners that there was an old lady who had lived there until very recently. Something of a character, she would chase people off the right of way running in front of her cottage and regularly go on foot to Chulmleigh, a very long walk, always refusing offers of lifts.

Mrs Betsy Gallup (yes – she is related to those Polls!) lives overlooking the Tamar Estuary near Bere Alston in a 16th-century

Not quite as derelict as you think, for there was a newspaper dated 1993 on the side of the seat.

farmhouse. Her pretty stone privy is covered in clematis in the spring. When we shone a torch into the hole, some 6 foot down we could see a stream gently running directly underneath in a very narrow stone gully. Although there is now modern plumbing this privy could still be used; in the old days its contents would have ended up in the Tamar though now it drains to a dispersal tank. Adjoining the farm was a large barn and the top floor used to be used as a doss house for the 'ladies' who came from Devonport Dockyard to supplement their trade by cherry picking in the days when the whole area was rich in cherry trees.

When we telephoned Pam Coleman she asked how we were

27

Off-centre seat – although there is now modern plumbing at the farm this privy could still be used. A narrow stone gully some 6 feet below carries a trickle down the hill to the Tamar.

going to get to her. 'By car of course' . . . 'Oh, no you won't unless you have a four wheel drive!' On a crisp, sunny and outstandingly clear October day we walked the dog to Bench Tor and after lunch at Hexworthy we set off with our Ordnance Survey reference. We walked miles across open moorland to find our goal. Our setter was the same size as the cavorting Dartmoor pony foals he kissed noses with on the way. Of all 'my' Devon privies this wins the prize for the best view from the seat, which is why they never put on a door! The original stream had been

The view from this seat is over fine rolling moorland, which must be why they never put on a door.

ingeniously diverted and the contents of the privy run gently down through to luxuriant reed beds. Built of solid granite, its slate roof is now sadly replaced with corrugated iron; somehow this didn't matter for the location was so magnificent. Bantams ran round the farmyard behind and 33 year old Rupert the donkey watched our every move from his half stable door.

Mrs Pauline Longhorn lives in Dolton, near Winkleigh and running beside a row of thatched cottages is a pretty little narrow lane. There resides a rather dilapidated rusty corrugated iron construction definitely of the bucket and chuck it variety. The corn apparently grew very much taller in the vicinity of the 'pit' just over the hedge. She tells a lovely story of when as children they used to be out of earshot of the adults and would sit and sing all the rude words they knew – their favourite song was 'bum, botty, wee wee, bum, botty, wee wee'. Mr Longhorn's parents also had a privy and one day the seat was left up and he fell in. Brother ran fast to the house, 'Mummy, Mummy – help! Ralph is in the shite!' Think on it – there were no washing machines in those days.

Cyril Rowland from South Molton left school in 1941 when he was 14 and was sent to work in a very good ironmonger's shop. It was here that he got to know about earth closet heavy galvanised pails which were regularly sold to country customers. Mr Rowland's father was a gamekeeper on a large wealthy country house estate and even though the owner was a rich man he didn't install a flush WC for the Rowland family and they had to make do with an Elsan. This was still in the old shed but was an advance on the pail! The Elsan consisted of a cylindrical bucket inserted into a box with an integral hinged seat. Into this bucket/drum was put a solution of Elsan chemical, mixed with water – about half a gallon in all – after each emptying, that is when the drum got 'dangerously' full. The ironmonger's stocked the Elsan in quarts, half gallons and gallons. When a

Gryff Thomas's Egyptian Temple Mau cat, Miw, waiting for rations through the wicket in a privy door that dates back to the Napoleonic Wars.

customer bought an Elsan it would be provided in a big box which would include the vent pipe. These vents would be between six to eight foot high and be inserted through the wall of the privy.

There is a small Welsh devil of a poet living in Topsham, Gryff Thomas, who wins my prize for the privy with the most unusual door, especially as so many didn't have any doors at all. Gryff lives in what was a pub (the Duke of Monmouth) until 1911, and the privy is now converted to a flusher. Its very special door, bought from Dartmoor Prison, contains a wicket through which the rations were passed to the prisoners.

Mrs Jean Green wrote to me from Exmouth to tell me about the delights of their 'Houses of Parliament'. When she was wearing her best Sunday clothes her black ankle strap shoes were perfect for doing tap dancing on the stone floor of their privy. She fancied herself as a budding star and would dance away to her heart's content. Her mother would fling open the door and say, 'You've not been sent down here to do that – you'll get constipated again if you don't go' ... this would mean a double dose of syrup of figs or rhubarb tea on the following Friday evening after her weekly bath in front of the fire.

From a Budleigh Salterton residential home Mrs Daphne Mears wrote to tell me that forty years ago she had been given a copy of that American classic *The Specialist*, written by Charles Sale. Published in 1930, it is still in print, in ten languages, with splendid illustrations by William Kermode (interesting name for an illustrator of privies?) and is surely immortal. So much does one of her grandsons enjoy the stories of that hilarious champion builder of privies, Lem Putt, she has had to promise to leave her copy to him when she leaves this world. Mrs Mears was a townie when she married and moved to the countryside and her brother-in-law always supplied them with magnificent sprouts

You never know where you might find a privy. Tucked away behind a high fence, and surrounded by modern bungalows in Plymstock, is what was originally a 16th-century Devon longhouse. Stone-built, with a slate roof, the old earth privy has the traditional sneck on the door and inside the strange luxury of two seat covers. The one in situ has a neat indented handle while the other is a plain wooden circle with no such facility. A privy puzzle?

and cauliflowers. When she learnt what the vegetable garden had been fertilised with she nearly had a fit. Her husband hadn't told her as, correctly, he thought she'd be so horrified she wouldn't eat the vegetables.

Mr Bowditch from Mutterton, near Cullompton, had a sentry box privy up the garden path, so called because of its shape. Next to the garden was a much lower lane. One night a gale sprang up and the wind uprooted the box and lifted it over the hedge, where it landed on its roof. All that remained was a square of concrete with a bucket in the middle – luckily no one was in residence (on duty?) at the time. The box was man-handled back over the hedge and reinstated by driving some posts into the ground and nailing the box to the posts – and there it remained for many more years.

Mrs Ann Adair, from Tavistock, told me the story of her father-in-law, who as a young apprentice painter and decorator was working at a grand house. In the back courtyard was an outside privy, complete with squares of newspaper hanging on a string, which he and his boss used when needed. One day he unlatched the privy door to find a young housemaid sitting there. He quickly closed the door and when she came out she was blushing furiously. He said 'You looked nice on the (w)hole' for which remark he was given the sack! He still swears he meant **whole**!

[3]

TWOS AND TRIBUMVIRATES

Our present day obsession with privacy would have seemed odd to the Romans for they were perfectly happy with their communal privies – a good place to meet friends and discuss the stories and news of the day.

Surely blessed by the Roman gods of ordure and convenience, Stercutius and Crepitus, the two and three-holers we discovered scattered throughout Devon were all magnificent. Multi-holers seemed so cosy and many people I spoke to talked of their chumminess – the romantic thought that the doubles might have been originally for honeymooners? Did they perhaps hold hands? In fact on a dark night, with no light except maybe a flickering candle, it was good, especially as a child, to have company down the garden path . . .

> There was a young fellow called Hyde
> Who fell down a privy and died
> His unfortunate brother
> Then fell down the other
> And now they're interred side by side.

Dartmoor proved to be a rich source of two-holers. One can only speculate why ... To the west, near Lewdown, we found a slightly scary two-seater right next to the millstream into which its contents used to flow, and on the other side of the moor, tucked away in the wilds beyond Widecombe-in-the-Moor, we were directed to an early 19th-century two-holer sitting on a bank above a stream. There was a pretty noisy constant flush some 7 feet below this wonder! Further east, near Hennock, the Seward family at Bullaton Farm, which is mentioned in the Domesday Book, are having their old barns and wonderful out-

This pretty little listed privy houses a pair of wooden seats and hides away at the back of a National Trust tenanted farmhouse in unspoilt countryside near Broadclyst. There is an off-centre door frame and the pyramidal roof is thatched with sedge. A quiet place to sit and contemplate.

36

This privy near Lewdown backs onto a millstream. Its exterior has been substantially restored though the interior has two sad little wooden keyhole seats and nowt else.

buildings gradually restored by Dartmoor National Park Authority. Here we were shown a splendid adult and child two-seater, reached by clambering up two huge chunks of Dartmoor granite.

Also up steps, this time a mounting block (for your needs when returning on horseback?), is a 6 foot wide two-holer at Broad-

37

The gap below the seats gives you a good view of the rushing stream underneath this listed two-holer near Widecombe-in-the-Moor, deep in the National Park.

hempston, near Totnes. This one backs onto the pigsty and is above a 4 or 5 foot drop to what was once a fast running stream.

At Dunkeswell, north of Honiton, a plank of wood forming the seat – with lids intact – of an adult and child two-holer has been reverently kept by Geoffrey Sworder, Chairman of the CPRE for Devon. The little thatched building where it was housed, again next to the pigsty, a common location, has sadly been demolished but has made way for a glorious herb garden. A

A rose-covered privy at the top of a mounting block at Broadhempston.

previous owner told the story of Thatcher Berry coming to re-do the roof and, after erecting all his scaffolding, realising that he had blocked off the only entrance to the privy – resulting in a not very comfortable, cross/cross-legged householder?

A tongue tickling word triumvirate, one of whose definitions is a group or set of three persons, especially three persons of author-ity or distinction *in any sphere*. Another definition, from Roman

39

This plank of wood is all that remains of an adult and child privy at Dunkeswell.

times, is the *position, office or function* of the triumviri. Could I dare invent 'tribumvirate'? I was looking for a word to describe the Devon three-holers without being too 'fanty sheeny' ('absurdly fanciful' for those who don't understand Devon dialect). Three cosy seats for Mum, Dad and the little one. Incidentally, whenever we found a two adults and one child privy the child seat was always on the right-hand side . . . Why?

On the outskirts of Newton Abbot is a listed 16th-century farmhouse and close to the house, set at the side of a huge walled garden, is a hipped-roofed three-holer. Only two seats were visible at first but a bit of delving around and we found the third much lower and smaller one. The ceiling was nearly 12 foot high and it was certainly the most spacious privy we visited.

It was a frosty morning when we went to see a grand two

A spacious listed three-seater with a 12 foot high ceiling at Newton Abbot. Spot the sneck!

adults and a child privy, next to a building of medieval origins near Ottery St Mary. It made one think! When the stream was in normal spate it was 6 feet below the bottoms but in times of flood, quite usual in that area, it must have provided natural cleansing . . .

South of Bishop's Tawton, high up above the river Taw, Brushford has a meticulously restored, and possibly once thatched, outbuilding containing an earth three-seater. The owner told me that the same family had lived there for over 400

The family seat(s) at Brushford, near Bishop's Tawton. The swallows have a nest in the top right-hand corner over the learning seat. Note the sneck!

Two adults and a child could sit together over this stream near Ottery St Mary.

years: 'The seat of the family remains, or rather the three seats. Two side by side plus a third of smaller calibre and lower altitude, possibly for the learners.'

[4]

PERSONAL PAPERS

In days of old when knights were bold
And paper weren't invented
They wiped their arse with tufts of grass
And went away contented.

(Playground ditty)

When you next pull a sheet of soft, even quilted, coloured, or patterned paper from a convenient roll, remember those privy users of not so long ago. Originally a handful of grass or dock leaves would suffice for a quick one behind the hedge. Ingenuity abounded – lettuce leaves, stones, shells of the right shape when you lived near the coast. Soft goose feathers for the ladies? A bunch of herbs? I wonder what name Devonians had for 'mempiria', which is a ball of rolled up hay!

'All good bum fodder'; such a descriptive name, for even the earliest junk mail, trashy literature and gutter newspapers. A 1660 satirical verse about the Rump (!) Parliament is titled *Bumm-Fodder; or Waste-Paper proper to wipe the nation's rump with, or your own*, and 'bumf' is still a much used word for tedious paperwork.

There is a reference in the Drake papers in the Devon Records Office, dated 10th January 1762, which states, 'The paper in the necessary house is the most soiled farthest from the door, it is owing to the dampness of the place.' One wonders what kind of paper? Twenty years earlier Lord Chesterfield quotes the story of a man who read Latin poems 'in the necessary house' and then made use of the pages he had read at each visit, slowly working through each book.

A tableau in Bygones Victorian Street in St Marychurch, Torquay.

A breakthrough in bottom wiping arrived in 1880 when British Patent Perforated Paper started to manufacture a roll, later to have the luxury of perforation. An alternative was the Automatic Toilet Paper Rack, for which an advertisement of 1906 reads: 'These papers are put in neat distributors for hanging on the wall; only one sheet of paper can be drawn at a time, and litter and waste are avoided'. One brand name for this system of folding was called the *Onliwon* . . .

All that was fine if you could afford it. Well into the second half of this century newspaper was the norm in 'end paper' (surely the forerunner of recycling). With no television, a daily newspaper was considered a must, and the chore of cutting up the squares invariably was delegated to the children – a real keep them quiet on Saturday morning job. Good sized squares of newspaper, pink interleaved if you had the *Financial Times*, a metal meat skewer to pierce a hole in the corner, a good bit of

The DRAYTON PAPER WORKS, Ltd.   21

"STANDARD."
Strong Paper (Unglazed).

DRAYTON MILL
"TOKIO QUALITY."
Very Thin Paper.
Wired for Hanging up.

South Park, Fulham, London, S.W.

Victorian ladies coyly referred to toilet paper as curling papers and from the many varieties of 'prize medal toilet papers' in this 1910 catalogue you could choose to purchase five hundred curling papers – Strong Paper (Unglazed) – for the princely sum of 6d!

binder twine or string threaded through and hung up on a nail ... and, I speak from experience, so often out of reach. The delight in being on your own in the privy and having reached a square of paper to find that it might be a salacious piece from something like the *News of the World*, a forbidden read for many children under a certain age, only to find someone had already taken the square containing the end of your story.

Hilda Forrest, now living in Sidmouth, remembers their small backyard in the 1920s. This contained an outbuilding which consisted of a coal house, an ash pit, the door being high in the wall into which all the household waste and ashes were placed and, next to the ash pit, the privy. This had a wooden seat with a round hole and a wooden lid and ran the width of the building; it was scrubbed so often that it was almost white. The wall dividing the ash pit from the privy did not reach the floor so all the fluid was absorbed into the ashes.

On Wednesdays the 'midden' men came to shovel everything out. They did this from the back street where there was a metal door which swung up and backwards. Powdered carbolic disinfectant was then strewn over the floor and for a short while it was almost pleasant to 'pay a visit'. Mrs Forrest remembers the possible forerunner of modern 'toilet tissue' – the smoothed out tissue paper that had been wrapped round the oranges and made a wonderful change from the usual squares of newspaper.

What Mrs Forrest didn't say but plenty of people had reminded me, was that the cheap pigments in this fruity 'foreign' paper could give your backside some lurid colouring ...

A lady in Woolfardisworthy, however, recalls the alternative treat of the good soft tissue of discarded dressmaking patterns.
Ian Maxted, the Devon County Local Studies Librarian, has made a life long study of toilet paper. In a wonderful article published in *The Ephemerist*, he uses the non-U term Toilet Paper in preference to the U term Lavatory Paper, since he says this is the way it was first designated in trade literature during Victorian

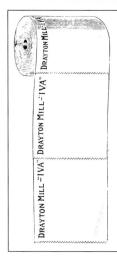

Can be had printed with **Customer's Own** **Name and Advertisement** on **each** piece, can also be banded with **Special** **Bands** in any design to suit Customer.

Prices and Full Particulars
- - *on application to* - -

The DRAYTON PAPER WORKS, Ltd.

South Park, Fulham, LONDON, S.W.

An advertising brainwave from 1910.

times. One firm, the Paper Cutting and Toilet Requisite Co, was not embarrassed to have its telegraphic address in 1895 as 'Toilet, London'.

Both world wars saw toilet paper used as propaganda. During the First World War Beecham's Pills sent paper to the front, reassuringly 'printed with clarified ink on non-irritant paper' and bearing cartoons and jokes including 'Take Beecham's Pills for active service'.

A roll of Second World War paper included a full-length portrait of Hitler with suitable captions, and Izal showed their patriotism with the following verse:

> Hitler now screams with impatience
> Our good health is proving a strain
> May he and his Axis relations
> Soon find themselves right down the drain.

The editions featuring portraits of Hitler were particularly popular . . .

[5]

PISSE-POTS

Presumptuous pisse-pot, how did'st thou offend?
Compelling females on their hams to bend?
To Kings and Queens we humbly bend the Knee
But Queens themselves are forced to Stoop to thee.
(The Pisse-Pots Farewell, 1697)

Until quite late in this century when most people finally had an indoor flusher at home, the chamber pot, jerry, potty or even gozunder – because it goes under the bed – was still a favourite for the 'easement of the night'.

From Ancient Greece onwards chamber pots were in use. By the 14th century potties were being made of every kind of material from tin and pewter and, it is rumoured, even gold. By the 18th century and its Age of Elegance, beautifully crafted pot cupboards were being designed by the great furniture makers such as Sheraton, Hepplewhite and Chippendale. You could then conceal your chamber pot in a wondrous piece of furniture, for example in the dining room; so convenient for the gentleman to use after drinking too much ale and port.

Gentlemen are fortunate in being born with a singular part of their anatomy that has been described as 'so useful on a picnic'. The ladies however, without such a convenient appendage, would be in quite a predicament and might carry their *bordalou* with them, perhaps discreetly concealed in a muff. Often these useful gravy-boat shaped utensils were made of fine porcelain and delicately decorated. Truly a portable pot!

'Beware of draughty privys and of pyssynne in draughts,' advised one Dr Boorde in the 15th century, 'and permyt no

50

This enchanting little chair could only be described as a child's commode and Mrs Gallup's children were potty trained with its help. It belonged to her husband's grandmother who died in 1921 in her eighties.

Quite what the Bishop is saying to the couple in bed, with their neat little jerry beside them in this medieval woodcut, beggars belief!

common pyssyng place about the house – and let the common house of easement to be over some water or else elongated from the house. Beware of emptyng pysse pottes, and pyssing in chymnes.' One hastens to add that those magnificent old, wide fireplaces had mounds of accumulated ash to piss on – this didn't mean down (or up) the 'chymnes'.

A 1738 Hogarth illustration showing the contents of the chamber pot hitting the wall above the open dentist's window (with open-mouthed patient in the chair) before showering the heads of those in the street below.

Emptying your potty has always been a problem – though it wasn't for poor Parson Woodforde in the Great Frost of 1785 for he wrote in his diary that his potty just froze under the bed. People living in towns, just emptied their chamber pots and kitchen slops from upstairs windows into the street. A shout of 'Gardy loo!' (*gardez l'eau*) was the only warning.

I often wonder whether that area of Staffordshire, The Potteries, is so called because of the smooth white china pots perfected there in the 18th century. Often with splendid applied decoration, and painted flowers, early chamber pots are now 'collectables'. Aristocratic families had their coats of arms emblazoned on the side of their potties and many others had rude rhymes and jokes, such as the little ditty written under a staring, open eye painted on the bottom of the pot:

> Use me well and keep me clean
> And I'll not tell
> What I have seen.

Some had famous figures – you could pee on Napoleon if you were so disposed, and even Hitler in the war years.

I own a rather clinical pottery object called 'The New Slipper Bed Pan' which now makes a good receptacle for a potted plant or two. The elegant script inside informs you that, 'This Slipper should be passed under the Patient in front between the legs. If a flannel cap is made for the blade fastened by strings under the handle considerable comfort will be afforded'. You bet!

In the 1930s Pat Pidler's father rented 160 acres of farmland from the Fortescue Estate in North Devon – for £160 a year. A cob and thatch Devon long house was their home. All his life Pat has gathered together and saved old tools, implements and

Pat Pidler, enthroned on the privy he rescued from his farm birthplace.

machinery, some of which he has used on the farm since his boy-hood days. The complete collection, including the old privy, can now be seen and enjoyed at The Milky Way tourist attraction outside Clovelly – a new form of farm diversification?

'As a collector of old things connected with farming, several years ago I went to a farm sale', Pat told me. 'After the main implements had been sold we all went into an old barn where oddments were on display for sale which included household goods including a water set which used to be used in the bed-room. It consisted of a large bowl and water jug, a soap dish, toothbrush pot and two charlie pots all sound with a harvest scene painted on them. The auctioneer's assistant was holding up the charlie pot for all to see and after my bid the auctioneer looked straight at me and said 'Name, Sir?' and I looked straight back at him and said 'Pidler'. After a short pause, a roar of laughter followed and after it had finished, with the assistant still holding the pot up, the auctioneer said 'Initial, Sir?' to which I replied 'P'. I don't believe the crowd could believe what they were hearing and they had another jolly good laugh.

'With a name like mine you need to laugh with everyone else. It doesn't worry me at all.'

Pee is a very cheap form of ammonia and a well known cure for chilblains was to soak your feet in a potful!

Synonym: 'to pee in the same pot' was to be of the same kind.

[6]

CREEPIES AND CRAWLIES

Anyone who has ever used a privy has memories of the animal and insect life lurking in the dark corners. Spiders, despite trying to keep the fly population in check, were not too welcoming and many people found it difficult to concentrate on the job in hand wondering where the cobweb ended. Daddy-long-legs of seemingly gigantic proportions were my personal nightmare. So often the privy was next to the hen house which might attract rats ... and the terror of strange squeaking and scratching noises in the dark and not knowing what you were going to find. Mrs Slade who lives in Pennycome Quick in Plymouth was brought up with twelve brothers and sisters on the Flete Estate. She has vivid memories of carrying the candle and matches down to their one-holer one night and finding all their hens roosting in there.

From Okehampton Mrs Gil Bach wrote to tell me that as a child she lived on a farm with a privy at the end of the garden. It was a single-seater with a tin roof and she can remember the rain pit-patting above while one was 'about one's business'. If they had a lot of company her father used to have to dig a hole in the garden to empty the bucket as the men only came once a week with their big smelly lorry. Their neighbours had a magnificent two-holer and Mrs Bach quite envied the companionship of the double seater when she was sitting on her own on a dull day. Her Aunty Dorrie had a privy and when she was little 'a rat jumped up as she sat down and attached itself to her delicate parts and Grandad had to knock it off with the broom handle . . .'

Mrs Lilian Crockett from Brixham reminisces about her early married life in the 1940s, remembering the owls swooping down as you walked to the privy in the dark, the good produce from

In order to reach this cob and stone delight, you have to cross the lane from an old farmhouse near Bridestowe. Almost shored up by an ancient yew tree, this one-holer is at the side of the old stables and you step down into it having walked past luxuriant runner beans – and a manure heap full of creepy crawlies.

the privy manured garden. Mrs K. Williams of Totnes has similar memories. Newly married in 1948, she and her husband rented a terraced house which was very nice but she hated the outside privy which was called a 'tippler'. It had a wooden seat from wall to wall with a hole in it. Below was a sort of steel rod with a pan in the middle. When this was full it tippled over into the drain below. One day when Mrs Williams was scrubbing the seat with bleach a rat shot out. The ratcatcher was called and a family of rats were found living in the drain. This was too much for the young newly-weds and they saved like mad and had a water toilet installed at the princely cost of £30.00. They were very proud of their new privy and all the neighbours came to admire it and were so impressed they all disposed of their 'tipplers' and installed more modern plumbing.

Hilda Forrest of Sidmouth recalls childhood visits to relatives who had a three-holer. In the winter, at the bottom of a dark and cold garden, the candle cast horrible shadows. 'I'm still frightened of the dark at 77', she says.

Mrs Maureen Lowe lives in an area of Exeter called Exwick with her husband and beautiful little granddaughter, Illea. When Mrs Lowe's mother, Irene Taylor, was still alive she used to enjoy reminiscing about the past and in particular their old privy, and often recalled taking the sink plunger on each visit because she hated spiders but didn't want to kill them. She would place the plunger over the spider and as soon as she had finished she would remove the plunger and make a run for it.

Her double privy had a piece of string which was attached to the latch on the door and if she let go whilst sitting there the door would spring outwards. She believed her love of singing was due to practice time on the privy. Later, as a teenager, she would climb onto the lean-to outside her bedroom window and run down to the privy where she would put on her make-up before going to her friend's house to don clothes and shoes she kept there for dancing. After the dance she would return the same way. Her parents never found out and her two sisters were sworn to secrecy.

When it came to emptying the privy buckets, Mrs Lowe's grandfather or her dad would dig holes in the garden and dispose

Mrs Maureen Lowe made this model with the help of her mother's privy recollections. It has all interior furniture intact, with even the necessary squares of newspaper hanging up – and is complete with a photograph of Vera Lynn on the back wall. Granddaughter Illea finds it all fascinating.

of the contents. They had some of the loveliest vegetables in the neighbourhood.

Winter wasn't too good – one needed a candle which flickered spookily, and you never loitered too long. A piece of doubled up newspaper would be folded and placed on the seat to prevent ice burns to the thighs as the seat was often frozen.

... AND BEARS

Lying in a fold of Dartmoor is Mary Tavy where John and Jill Lamerton live in a pretty long white cottage. This was probably once three mineworkers' cottages for at one end of the village is Wheal Friendship, formerly one of the most productive copper mines. John and Jill can proudly boast *three* privies, a stone-built one across the orchard being the *pièce de résistance*. As we walked up the steep hill towards the honeysuckle, japonica and blackberry covered building on our late-summer visit, we passed laden apple trees each of them bizarrely populated with teddy bears! The Lamertons reckon the bears frighten off the apple-eating birds, but the now obsolete privy has been home to gold-finches in the japonica and blue tits nest in the crevices of the

The Lamertons' Mary Tavy privy, no longer in use but home to nesting gold-finches and blue tits.

stones. A true conservationist, John spent much of his working life with the Nature Conservancy (now called English Nature). After home-made carrot cake for tea, we were given a punnet of delicious wineberries to take home, grown in the splendid vegetable patch by the other privies.

...NOT TO MENTION COWS

Val Holder from Torquay used to compose splendid little ditties like this one for her late husband while she was preparing his lunch!

My Missus has got it at last –
The New Bath in upstairs.
This past thirty year her kept on at me,
Like an itch from an unfound flea.
I b'aint one for lightning decisions
Like them chaps up at County Hall.
I takes me time and ruminates
Whilst considering pros and cons.
Us has nice old place down orchard
With new galvanised bucket and all,
A warm wooden seat with hole in
And a bit of old rug on the floor.
'Tis always a pleasure to go down there
And meditate for a while –
I smokes me pipe, then catch up with the news
From the squares of old print
Tied up good and neat – hanging from nail in the wall.
The gap in the door is just enough
To admire the lovely view,
Which changes according to season –
'Cept last winter it blew
And near lifted me off the seat

When the wind got round the East.
There's a little window at the back
To get the right ventilation.
One day I was sitting in there
When I had the queerest sensation.
I could hear the heavy breathing
Then hot breath on the back of me neck
And rattle of a chain
As the 'Thing' shook its head . . .
'Tis old Ghost for sure, think I –
'Oh God, please don't let me die
With me trousers down –
I've been private all me life
As my Missus will testify.'
When I turned me head I had to laugh –
Weren't no ghost but our old cow
With head stuck through window –
She couldn't get out no how!
I reckon I'll stick to my throne
With its memories of bygone years.
I'll leave they new fangled bathrooms
To Missus and them that likes chrome.
T'will be useful when Vicar calls . . .
But I know where I feels at home.

[7]

PRIVY EMPTYING
OR
DISPATCH OF BUSINESS

In Mr Pepys' time there was a 'nightman and poleman' called Henry Hastings whose engraved trade card, now kept in a museum, advertised 'the new invented machine carts for the quick dispatch of Business' . . .

―――――――

What strange things statistics are! Someone has worked out that, in a lifetime of 65 years, an individual produces 4 tons of excrement and approximately $7\frac{1}{2}$ thousand gallons of urine. But where is this all to go? It used to be fine in rural Devon, for an acre of land would accommodate the waste of approximately 250 people – a valuable and organic soil fertiliser for farmland, gardens, and allotments. As the population increased in towns, however, so did the often smelly problem of waste disposal.

The successors to the medieval gongfermors were the night cart men who used to arrive in their horsedrawn open cart, and with the advent of the motor, an elliptical shaped metal tanker. Even today in Devon if you are not 'on the mains' and your cesspit contents are not breaking down naturally, the modern equivalent of the honey cart will have to come and pump the excess away, but in daylight! Not so our gentlemen of the night, the Moonlight Men, sometimes with handkerchiefs tied bandit-style round their faces, with magical names for their carts such as the Iron Duke, the Lavender Cart, the Dunnekin Drag, the Violet Wagon, the Honey Wagon. How much more romantic than the 'night soil collection vehicle'. You tightly closed all windows on collection night for the smell could be none too sweet. It

Gentlemen of the night. (BBC Hulton Picture Library from *The Complete Loo* by Roger Kilroy, Victor Gollancz 1948).

was hard on those who had to have the buckets carried through the house.

Mrs Aldridge from Huntsham, near Tiverton, didn't have a flush loo in the estate cottages they lived in until the late 1970s and prior to that they had to carry the full bucket, looking carefully left and right before venturing to cross the road to the gardens. When they lived in an old farm cottage at Uplowman they had to cross a footbridge to the privy as the garden was across the wide stream. Being the eldest girl she very often had to take the younger members of the family to the privy after dark, carrying a candle in a jar for light. They would all tell frightening tales if someone was taking too long because they wanted to get back indoors in the warm. One of the sisters always used to go to the privy with a book, to avoid having to wash the dishes. When her parents lived in a mill cottage at Sampford Peverell they had a two-holer over the millstream and her father used to boast that it was his first flush WC as he got a free wash when the stream was in full flow.

When Mrs Aldridge married in 1942 their privies were at the top of steep gardens with the wash houses in front and the pig houses behind. Mrs Aldridge described her husband as 'taking out three pits for the job'. They used the old bucket for years until the chemical toilet came in – and though it still had to be emptied it wasn't quite so smelly. She tells the story of her husband out harvesting and the children coming in to tell her that the bucket was full and about to overflow. She put the children to bed, went outside and 'took out the three pits'. One filled, then the second, then the third – and then overflowed across the bottom path, down the old stone wall into their cobbled backyard. She was still brooming away the mess when her husband returned and explained that she was supposed to give the liquid time to soak away first – too late – it was the first and last time she tried to do that job!

Mrs Aldridge's letter was full of horror stories – making sure there were no spiders before one lifted the seat and remembering her sister who now lives in Australia and has to cope with the enormous red spiders in the dunnies out there. Mrs Aldridge didn't think I would find any privies left to photograph and that the seats and buckets would all be gone. Little did she know!

Mrs Alice Kemp of Moretonhampstead was in the ATS during the war and on their gunsite 'the bucket' was collected twice a day by an old man with a pony and cart. The Lavender Cart had a metal drum and contents splashed everywhere, she remembers.

It paid to be friends with your night cart man and there is many a story of a bottle of beer or a present of eggs being left to sweeten his unenviable job. Here is one such tale:

It was Christmas and the Depression and the prospect of feeding the family did not look good until a local farmer gave them a live turkey as a thank you for past kindnesses. The turkey was kept in the back garden until a few days before the Christmas feast – no fridges in those days. A local fox was causing havoc and the family felt it would be sensible, for safety's sake, to keep the turkey in the only safe place they had, the privy, for its last few nights. On the second night the poor old turkey disappeared. Nobody could understand how because the door to the privy was still on its latch or sneck. A week after Christmas a member of the family met 'George the Lavender Man' who profoundly thanked him for his generous Christmas present. George had found the turkey asleep on the seat of the privy when he made his last 'collection' before the holiday. It was traditional to leave a Christmas box for the night cart man . . .

Brian Hardiman from Withycombe Raleigh remembers when he was a child on Sunday school outings and how they used to go to a house where there was a family with thirteen children and – presumably for this reason – an (earth) three holer. The father cleaned the privy out with a very long handled ladle

A traditional 'shittus scoop' once used by local councils on their honey cart emptying sessions.

which a member of the family still has as a reminder of the 'good old days'.

Of course, some privies did not have to be emptied . . .

Up in North Devon not too far from South Molton we took a mile-long track across the open fields to Muckford – the Mucky Ford – once probably a very appropriate name. Here the privy with its two-hole seat has pride of place at the rear of an early 19th-century farmhouse overlooking unspoilt countryside. When running water, and therefore an inside lavatory, was installed the then tenant farmer flatly refused to use it and continued to use her outside privy. Half a mile up the hill from the farm the stream was dammed, and a trickle would run down past the side of the buildings into a pond, which in turn fed the stream under the privy, and then naturally down the field to a stream called the Crooked Oak.

And many, too, were the stories about flourishing gardens:

Mary Atkins went to stay with her sister and family in a tied cottage at Morebath in 1950. Their privy was part of a pigsty and consisted of a bucket covered by a wooden table with a hole in the middle. Next to the privy was a pile of hay and when you had used the bucket you put a handful of the hay on top. The bucket was only emptied when the hay reached your bottom. Her brother in law would then dig a ditch and empty the contents in for future fertiliser and he was renowned for the best vegetables in Morebath. Mrs Atkins' children and grandchildren are horrified by this recollection.

When Mr George West telephoned I knew from his voice that it would be well worth visiting him at Brightly, just north of Okehampton. We finally got there on a damp November afternoon when, as Mrs West said, 'there had even been a skitter of snow'.

Mr West wasn't at home but his wife entertained us warmly with her infectious laugh and smile. Five years ago, the Wests moved into what used to be Mrs West's mother's old cottage, one of a terrace backing right onto the mill stream. In this case the three privies were not built over the stream, but across the road in a long row at one side of the lush vegetable garden. Their landlord also had a privy round the corner – it was bigger as he had farther to walk! A real delight was at last finding a genuine privy bucket. Giggling, Mrs West led us to the greenhouse to show us the unusual late flowering mauve chrysanthemums now growing in it. Stuck in the earth at the side was a label reading AFLM. Mrs West laughed again for her Auntie had given her a cutting (did she really say 50 years ago?) and of course the initials stood for Auntie Flo's Late Mauve.

My stepfather always kept a tall white enamel jug in our privy into which the men were requested to pee. This was used to water the tomatoes – and what a crop we used to grow. Everywhere now folk want organic foods but just think when you next buy expensive liquid fertiliser how much more satisfying it would be if you had produced it yourself! A vegetarian lady from Dittisham, that famous plum growing area, reckoned that anything that passed through her must be fit for the compost, and said, 'what comes out of bums was good for plums' . . .

THE SHIT SHIP

When you drive on the M5 bridge over the river Exe to and from South Devon and beyond, think of a classic little tanker that used to be officially known as the 'SW2'. For thirty-five years this specially built 122 foot long vessel has carried Exeter's sludge out to sea from the treatment works at Countess Wear (which also became the ship's name in 1974 though locally she is known affectionately as The Shit Ship). She navigates the $1\frac{1}{2}$

The 'SW2' or *Countess Wear* in the Exeter Canal at Turf Lock heading back to the sewage works for her next load. EC regulations have sounded her death knell and she goes the way of the privies. (Photo courtesy of Jon Bennett)

miles of Britain's oldest ship canal, under the M5, to the early 19th-century Turf Hotel and its sea lock. Down the Exe she sails past Dawlish Warren and Exmouth, and when six miles out to sea she has the capacity to dump her 300 tonne cargo overboard in thirty minutes and return home on the same tide. Not so many years ago she used to deliver beer and supplies to the Turf Hotel as she went through the lock, but the Nanny State stopped that. Representing the last commercial traffic on the canal, the Countess is a remnant of 400 years of trade with the Port of Exeter and the last cargo carrying vessel on an estuary rich in maritime history.

A POLICEMAN'S LOT

Now in her 80s, Mrs Vera Bartlett, whose father was in the Devon Police, remembers living in police houses at Tedburn St Mary, Milton Abbot, then Horns Cross in North Devon, all of them with privies which had to be emptied. By the time she was sixteen her family had moved to Bideford and grandly had electric light, running water and an upstairs and a downstairs lavatory. Eventually she too married a policeman and they went to live in Sidbury, and then after the war in Culmstock, then to Woolacombe – all of them with bottom of the garden privies again! As she said, 'A policeman's lot was not always an easy one'.

[8]

WARTIME WOES

Mike Beeston is a splendid pilot who jointly runs Exeter Air Training School and here he relates the story told him by a friend, Mary Carnall (née Morgan), who lives in Clyst Honiton, very near Exeter Airport: '1941 and England was at war and the airport was in the hands of the Royal Air Force. Once a small private aerodrome it had become RAF Exeter and was now a very active fighter station playing host to squadrons of Hurricanes and Spitfires as well as pilots from other countries, some of them in what had become Nazi occupied Europe. The British fighters were employed in a defensive role to protect the South West from German bombers that regularly attacked the cities and airfields of Exeter and Plymouth.

'Mary's family lived in a tied cottage which was situated perilously close to the north western end of Exeter's runway 31. As this was directly in line with aircraft both taking off and landing, the area was known as the "overshoot" for obvious reasons.

'Hayes Cottage, in common with many of its type, had no mains electricity or running water but there was a yard with a well and hand pump, and a shed known as the linney with a privy attached at the rear. The privy had a hinged wooden seat under which stood a bucket that required regular emptying. Toilet paper was made up from old newspapers cut into squares, piled one on top of the other with a hole punched in one corner for string to be threaded through, then hung onto the door ready for use. Mary and her brother John would amuse themselves by removing the string and attempting to piece together the pages rather like a jigsaw puzzle.

'The noise of the air raid sirens in Exeter could be heard clearly by the residents of Clyst Honiton and this was the signal for John and Mary to leave their beds and make a dash for cover

– which meant sheltering in the privy until the "all clear" siren. Their father refused to let the Luftwaffe spoil a good night's sleep and decided to stay in his bed.

'As the raids intensified an orange glow could be seen over the city as it burned and often the allied fighters returning to the airfield were short of fuel and ammunition and the Morgan children watched them being chased and strafed by German aircraft as they were landing.

'Eventually due to their vulnerability the family would stay the night with friends in the more remote village of Broadclyst, a couple of miles to the north and considerably safer. They would return to their cottage every morning for breakfast, before the children walked the further half mile to the village school in Clyst Honiton.

'Returning home one morning after an air raid, the family were confronted by the sight of their cottage without its roof and windows. Hayes Cottage had taken a direct hit and was gutted though fortunately no one was in residence at the time. Mary walked across the yard to the privy only to find the wooden seat peppered with bullet holes.

'Fortunately Hayes Farm survived and is still a working farm, though sadly the cottage was damaged beyond repair and had to be demolished.

'It seems not only bombs rained down that night back in 1941 but a little luck too!'

Mrs Drake, who now lives in Dawlish, was brought up on a farm between Broadclyst and Whimple. They had no electricity and their privy was at the bottom of the garden. It was built of galvanised iron and contained a lovely solid wood seat. The bucket was emptied each day, in a pit dug on nearby waste land and then covered with ashes from the kitchen range. During the war she took in land army girls, and remembers two girls in particular who she describes as 'middle class but very sweet'. The farm was only two fields away from Exeter Airport as the crow flies and obviously that is where the girls found their boy friends. One evening when the young men were visiting, one of them had occasion to use the privy and they decided to frighten him by throwing a brick on the roof. Poor chap obviously thought it was an air raid and shot out of the privy with his trousers down. He wasn't at all pleased but then saw the funny side of it. Mrs Drake remembers how it wasn't all doom and gloom in the war years for they made their own fun. Bombs were being dropped all around them and when they saw the craters in the mornings they felt just lucky to be alive.

Mrs Gallup was in the ATS during the war and told us the fearful tale of the latrine hut with a dozen seats in a long row with only the minimum privacy door in front of each cubicle. Under every hole in the long row was a bucket and behind that a wooden flap in order for the buckets to be collected and emptied. Waking very early one morning with a bad upset tummy she donned her gumboots and raincoat and rushed to the latrine block which she knew at that time of the morning would be quiet and moderately private. Just as she sat down there was the most fearful racket and from behind the block a hand took the bucket from underneath her, emptied it and put it back. She never knew till then what strong sphincter muscles she owned!

Miss Patricia Lawrence of Exmouth 'had a privy halfway down the garden though it seemed further away as the cottage was built on the side of a hill with the garden at roof level; after going up the steps from the yard one's only sight of the house was the blank wall of the gable end giving a "cut off" feeling. During the war Mother had gone up alone for a final visit on a summer evening when the light was fading. At that time we had a thick double row of runner beans flanking the path leading to the privy. From the middle of the beans a man arose, raised his forage cap, said "Home Guard manoeuvres Ma'am" and resumed his position. Poor Mother had to continue on even though, in those days, people were bashful about such things. My father having been more or less crippled in an accident, and my mother not being strong, the task of emptying the bucket fell to us older girls; in the winter this would have to be done after dark of course, so we would chant lines from "The Burial of Sir John More at Corunna" while doing it – teenagers have an odd sense of humour!'

Imagine, as an airman during the war, being all buttoned up in your flying suit and strapped in your seat and wanting to pee. Simple solution was a milk bottle.

We were told the story of a Commanding Officer who simply refused to have latrines on the air station built in the usual row with no privacy ... so 'à la Knights of the Round Table' they were built in a circle with everyone sitting looking outwards.

Arthur Pike from Tiverton vividly remembers having been brought up with modern luxuries in the 1920s and then being sent to stay with his farming grandparents in the holidays. There was a form of plumbing on the farm for the women but the men had to put their boots on in order to go down to the privy. Mind you, he said, it was probably a useful preparation for a soldier's life in India and Burma!

[9]

PUBLIC PRIVIES

In days gone by the wealthy man might have had the luxury of an indoor 'house of easement' with even a baize cover for the seat. He might, too, have spent money on 'chamber pottes' for his household; but his methods of sewage disposal were as primitive as those of the lowliest cottager. Luckily for the grand families they had more space and were possibly able to avoid the dangers of pestilence raging in overflowing gutters in the narrow streets. In London, for example, in the year after the Armada the Fleet river was cleansed and scoured, but before long, thanks to the 'casting of soilage into the stream' it had become 'worse cloyed and choken then ever it was before'. Many a town and even rural leat would have been the same right up to the 19th century.

Down in Devon matters were apparently *slightly* more civilised for the city fathers of Exeter had provided public latrines before 1467, over the mill-leats in the lower part of the town. On the old Exe Bridge 'there was an open space in the centre of the bridge with a doorway and a flight of steps that led to a long vaulted room, commonly called the Pixey or Fairy House'!

Other records show that in 1568 the City Chamber ordered that 'there shall be three common jakes or widraughtes made within the City, viz one at Frenhay, and one at the town hall in St Paul's Parish (ie The Guildhall) and the third about the Water Gate.' On a map of the period you can see where the Water Gate jakes was. There was a stream running down Coombe Street, which went through a hole in the City Wall, and this would have acted as a flush. The seats would have been on top of the City Wall and behind the old Custom House you can still see a part of the arch through which this stream ran. A clue to the poor sanitation of the time is the name of the stream

Didn't know what to make of this one! An interesting receptacle found at Chulmleigh.

that rose at the end of Sidwell Street and ran past St Leonard's church into the river Exe. For hundreds of years this was called the Shitbrook but this descriptive Saxon-named stream was lost when it was covered in and converted to a storm sewer during the 1840s.

It was cholera that forced the first Public Health Act in 1848, when Lord Shaftesbury became that 'ameliorater of the condition of the lower classes'. When one room could contain a family in each corner and there was a cellar with a cesspool immediately below the boarded floor it was not surprising that life expectancy, particularly of children, was so short.

Devon still has the largest amount of outside flushers; out of our 690 primary schools, an astonishing 46 of them, mainly in rural areas.

South Molton Infants School in North Devon has 160 pupils aged between four and seven who still have to use outside loos. Their headmistress, Pam Cruse, feels it is totally unacceptable that this should be so at the end of the 20th century. 'It might have been different 50 years ago when some children had to go outside at home to use the toilet but there aren't any homes left like that now and haven't been for many years,' she said. 'Why should children therefore be expected to put up with such facilities when they go to school?' Pam told me about North Molton Village Hall, where not so very long ago the stream directly under the overhanging outside 'conveniences' ran straight down to the village pond. Kids would put a little flag on various 'objects' and see which one reached the pond first . . . an older version of 'pooh sticks'?

Endacott House in the medieval stannary town of Chagford was previously called St Catherines Guild Hall and then the British Legion Hall and I dare say a few other things as well. Lurking behind this Poor House, and then school, is a row of privies. The fronts are strangely modernised (*top*) but behind the doors are little privies (*bottom*) in varying sizes with the stream running underneath.

Huge onions are drying in the foreground of this L shaped privy in Chulm-leigh and there is a rusty mousetrap hanging from the door frame.

In Chulmleigh, North Devon we met James Ravilious, a leading contemporary landscape photographer, who spent 17 years compiling the Beaford Archive at the Beaford Arts Centre. This collection of photographs, almost the largest of its kind in Europe, is of the utmost importance to anyone interested in life in the countryside over the past 150 years, a magnificent in-depth visual record of rural traditions that are fast fading from view. Using the sophisticated computerised records we tried to work out under what category you would file a photograph of a privy. Toilets? Lavatories? We found some splendid ones filed under goats coming out of privies. James led us round the corner from his home to what was once one of the seven pubs in the town (today there are only three) – an old coaching inn that is now a private house. The Black Horse apparently achieved such a bad name for rowdiness because of the clientele of navvies building the Exeter to Barnstaple railway that in 1860 the name was changed to the White Hart. In a tiled barn at the back, we found an L shaped privy, with a main drain running under-neath. The seats were so close together that when two were sitting their knees would touch.

***

'In order to attract a better class of person' a certain Town Council in the West Country once voted to replace the words *Men* and *Women* on their public conveniences with *Ladies* and *Gentlemen* . . .

***

Stranded between the railway and the bypass east of Newton Abbot is the early 17th-century Forde House, once a manor belonging to Torre Abbey and now owned by Teignbridge District Council. The Great Chamber, barrel vaulted and decorated with spectacular plasterwork, was officially re-opened

Forde House privy lies over a clogged up stream; the tiled roof is in comparatively good condition, but the interior has totally gone to pot. It would be good if Teignbridge District Council could find the money to restore her before she totally disintegrates. The doves might appreciate it.

after extensive restoration, by HM The Queen and Prince Philip in the 1980s. The then Chairman of the Council, the late Councillor Pike proudly showed Her Majesty the Great Chamber and said, in his broad Devon accent, 'And this is where I doos my business.' The other business was performed in a pretty, probably two-, if not more, holer in the grounds.

All over Europe you can now find the terrifying, for me, APCs or 'Automated Public Conveniences'. Vandal proof and spotlessly hygienic they may be but the first time I used one, and the need to go was paramount, I honestly didn't think I would ever get out alive. It was the early 70s, we were about to join a long car ferry queue; I put my coin in the slot and the door swished open. Once inside I felt big brother was watching me for the door swung shut with a locking click. I didn't know it was my weight on the floor. Relief at last and then the washbasin automatically produced soap and water followed by hot air to dry my hands. With the buzzes, hums and clicks I nervously thought it might give me a shower into the bargain. When I eventually found the way out there was a discreet hiss as the lavatory bowl retracted to be cleaned, disinfected and air dried, followed by a spray clean of the floor. Oh give me back my cosy privy with a paraffin lamp and a book any day.

A shy young couple had been shown round a Devon cottage they were interested in buying. When they returned home, however, they remembered they hadn't noticed any 'facilities' and wrote to ask where the WC was. Under some misapprehension, the owner of the cottage replied:

'The nearest WC is situated in the next village, a pleasant five mile walk away but unfortunate if you are in the habit of going regularly. Sadly owing to vandalism we have to keep it locked and it is only open once a month so one can only use the facilities on a rota system. There are a lot of visitors in the tourist season and I would therefore advise you to get there early. Although there is accommodation for 100 people, the last time my wife attended (and she had not been for some months) she had to stand the whole time. The old wooden seats were in a bad state of repair and have been replaced with plush velvet ones which makes the whole proceedings more comfortable for those who wish to sit. I should be pleased to reserve you both a seat and be the first to take you to them. The visiting Minister stands in full view of everyone so it is not difficult to hear him. I must add that the place is very calming and those who visit leave something behind and come away much relieved. There are always hymn sheets provided for your personal use.'

Oh well . . . it makes a good story and has been told to me in three slightly different versions – there must be an awful lot of Wesleyan Chapels around!

Mary Mountain lives in Kenn, outside Exeter, and her sons have bought her a typewriter. The following little poem about an all-too-public privy is one of the results:

Bucket Loo
A little gang of cheeky kids often would meet
We would wait for the occupant to settle on the seat
Then through the latch hold we would peep
To see the occupant's surprise, but some had gone to sleep.
We would gang up outside the door
To hear the bucket music play,
Then with a loud roar of laughter
We would all run away.
The occupant would storm in a very angry mood:
You cheeky little devils, you are very, very rude.

[1 0]

PRIVIES TODAY

So many Devon privies are gems of architecture in their own right and need to be treasured. It was a delight as I criss-crossed the county, to keep finding little dunnekins that may not be used for their original function but nevertheless are appreciated.

Twenty-three miles up the river Tamar from Plymouth lies the inland port of Morwellham. From the Middle Ages it was the port for the stannary town of Tavistock but its great period of

Alfie, the author's setter, approaches one of the restored semi-detached privies at Morwellham. The notice on the gate says 'Do not feed the animals' – but there wasn't a pig in residence that day.

Why did the lid have a chain? I couldn't decide if this was original or whether it was to stop Morwellham visitors taking home a keepsake.

prosperity arrived in the 1850s when the copper mines at Devon Great Consols boomed.

The boom caused a growing housing crisis and architect-surveyor Theophilus Jones (to my delight I discovered he too was Anglesey born) wrote, 'such is the want of cottage accommodation that ... a room about 14 feet by 12 feet in the neighbourhood is occupied by a man, his wife, six children, and four single men lodgers.' One of the key figures engaged by the Duke of Bedford's Estates, Theophilus was as keen as the Duke himself to improve local living conditions. Model cottages were built to a high standard, for the time; some were erected as terraces whilst others were semi-detached. Most had two rooms downstairs and two or three bedrooms upstairs. A design specification of 1849 states that outside there must be 'a pigsty and ashpit, a drying ground and a garden'. Each cottage could be built for the princely sum of £89 7s 5d.

Once one of the richest sources of copper in the world, but soon exhausted, the mines and the quay that served them fell into disuse. Now restored, Morwellham Quay is a thriving tourist area where you can see the old copper mines and the port, visit the museums, Victorian workshops, see shire horses and farm animals, amongst other attractions. You will find restored semi-detached privies and another by the Lime Burner's Cottage and if you want any information the warm and welcoming staff, dressed in period costume, are always on hand to help.

All we had to go on was a map reference. Many of the privy sites on Dartmoor had led us to wild and wonderful areas we didn't even know existed. On the rolling hillsides above Widecombe we found the man we were looking for. We spotted his modern cowboy's quad bike, parked by the newly repaired stone walls and guarded by a gentle collie. Five hundred yards down the hill, surrounded by inquisitive red brown cows, he was mending a fence. 'Are you Peter?' 'We are all called Peter round here,' was his reply. 'Do you have a privy?' 'You have come to the right place – retrace your steps a mile to the farm and my wife will show you.' His wife turned out to be a friend of my husband from teenage days – another very welcome surprise on our privy quest!

The privy in question lies over a now dry leat which used to run from the pond and weir. Built of Dartmoor granite, with a standing stone (or was it an old granite gatepost?) as guard, this two-holer was once thatched – these days she has a smart tiled roof and a new door and has come into her own again as a useful store shed.

This Widecombe two-holer has lost its thatch and seats but is a good store shed – with its watching standing stone.

When is a privy not a privy? At Dunsford in the Teign valley, not far from Steps Bridge, Maggie Morgan described their home as 'a bungalow built on top of a one hundred year old basement barn'. The garden at the back used to be the village bowling green. At the side of the garden, snuggling behind a pavilion, was a small post with a notice saying 'Gents'. At the end of a very narrow shed stood an ordinary standard china pedestal with seat and cover. But it wasn't plumbed in and just emptied straight into the fast gurgling stream beneath! Obviously no longer in use, and neither sadly is the bowling green. A pair of green woodpeckers were advertising their presence with a ringing series of laughing 'klee-klee-klee' notes in between drilling happily into the nearby telegraph pole.

There has been a village at Sidbury since Saxon times and here we found a little earth privy belonging to a 400 year old house that was once a goat farm. Although the indoor 'furniture' had long since gone it sported a fine VHF aerial. Apparently the house once belonged to an ex-Chief Constable. On his retirement the only way he could keep in touch with his old force – from the bottom of a very deep valley – was to have the VHF aerial installed. One is left in little doubt about where he sat to listen in.

YOU CAN TELL A LOT FROM A LOO ...

Children always seem fascinated with lavatories ... there seems to be a stage in all our lives when we begged, in strange houses, to go. 'But you've just been,' the grown ups would say – but you wanted to see if the plumbing was different from that at home. Did they have a cold and draughty functional outside lav, or a grand floral bowl or a huge mahogany seat, a carpeted and 'modern sprayed' papered emporium with matching towels, soap, and paper? An all pervading pong of the Body Shop? Would it just have crackly Bronco?

Would it have a soft imitation lambswool cover on the seat and a knitted dancing girl with a swirly skirt to cover the loo roll? Would it be spartan and Nordicly hygienic, or would it have a row of wellington boots and gardening gear? Or would it be a homely privy, hopefully smothered in ivy and roses!

You visit a house for the first time and you have exhausted all the questions you feel you can politely ask your host but it is only

These semi-detached privies belong to John and Jill Lamerton in Mary Tavy. Now useful garden sheds, they nestle snugly at the very top of the luxuriant vegetable garden.

when at last you are asked if you would like to use the bathroom (or one of those other strange euphemisms) that you possibly learn more of the character of the household. There you might find old school photographs, the odd framed faintly vulgar poem, the potted papyrus, the naughty seaside postcards, a photograph or two of your host shaking hands with someone famous, perhaps even royalty.

Amongst my favourites was the loo in the all girl household for under the seat was written, 'Goody goody, MEN in the house'.

[11]

END PIECE

Mary Mountain from Kenn provides a nostalgic summing up:

At the bottom of the garden
Stood a little wooden shed
With a pile of cut up newspapers
And when on the wooden seat you sat, this is what you read.
But to find out only half a story was no laugh
Because the one in front of you had used the other half.
The perfume of Jeyes fluid covered a multitude of sins.
Just a wooden latch upon the door to keep us in
With white washed walls
And creosote on the door
No lights on the ceiling
Plain concrete on the floor.
Too far and cold to walk at night
To this little garden shed
So you would find a chamber pot
Underneath your bed.
On the darkest night the bucket seemed to do a walk
What the neighbours did not see
Meant the neighbours wouldn't talk
For in the good old days nothing went to waste
We would fertilise the garden with a dignifying haste.
We did not need water to flush the waste away,
For recycling always was, the order of the day.

THE VERY LAST WORD

Mary also told me a little story (I heard three variations on this theme!) about a builder who asked to use their privy. He seemed to have been gone for a long time and her father went to see what had happened to him. There was the builder wielding a long batten with a nail on the end, trying to hook his coat, which had fallen into the bucket. Father told him not to bother for the coat would now be of no use. The builder replied, 'I know that, but my lunch is in the pocket.'

A Privy By Any Other Name

The thesaurus is confusing enough: Toilet – a noun. Lavatory, bathroom, WC, public convenience, ladies' room, powder room, convenience, out-house, urinal, latrine, and PRIVY! Imagine trying to learn English and coming across even half a dozen of the following extraordinary euphemisms . . . and I bet I've left somebody's favourite description out.

A 'certain' place
Aster room
Backhouse
Biffy
Bog/Boghouse
Bombay
Bush
Chamberlain pianos (row of
    buckets)
Chamber of Commerce
Chuggie
Closet
Comfort station
Craphouse
Crapper
Crapping castle
Dike
Dinkum-dunnies
Doneks
Dubs
Duffs
Dunnekin
Garden loo
Garderobe

Gong house
Gong
Go and have a Jimmy Riddle
Go and have a Tom Tit
Going to pick daisies
Going to see a man about a
    dog
Going to stack the tools
Going to the George
Going to the groves
Going to where the wind is
    always blowing
Grots
Heads
Here is are
Holy of Holies
Honk
House of Commons
House of Office
Houses of Parliament
Hum
Jakes
Jam pot
Jerry-come-tumble

Jericho
John
Karzi
Klondike
Larty
Latrine
Lats
Library
Little house
Long drop
Loo
My aunt's/uncle's
Necessary
Nessy
Netty
Out the back
Petty
Place of easement
Place of repose
Place of retirement
Ping pong house
Reading room
Round the back
Sammy
Shants
Shithouse (et al!)
Shooting gallery
Shot tower
Slash house
Smallest room
Sociable
Sunkie
Tandem (two-holer)
The End

Thinking house
The opportunity
Throne room
Thunderbox
The usual offices
Ty bach (Welsh for 'little house')
Wee house
Watering hole
Whatchamacallit
Widdlehouse
Windsor Castle
'Yer Tiz'
You know where
Whare-iti (Maori for 'little house')

Requests for the WC seem to be even more complex:
Adam & Eve
Chain of events
Just off to:
    point Percy at the Pommie porcelain (Aussie!)
    powder my nose
    shake hands with my best friend
    telephone Hitler
    water the horses
The penny house
The plumbing
The urinal
Waterloo
Umtag (Russian WC)